The OLD-TIME RELIGION

SACRED PIANO SOLOS
Rebecca Bonam

Contributing Editors
Duane Ream
Alice Gingery

Typographer
Alan Lohr

Design
Chris Hartzler

SOUNDFORTH
Traditional music for today's ministry

REBECCA BONAM

Since she was old enough to sit in church services and be transfixed by the piano, Rebecca Bonam wanted to "play all over those keys and create beautiful sounds." She spent hours at an overturned washtub in her back yard, pretending to play as the church pianist did. At six, she had her first official music lessons. Despite her great desire to play, Rebecca worried that she "would never be able to understand the keyboard" and even begged her parents not to make her take lessons.

Thankful now that her parents did not listen to her, Rebecca recalls her struggle with the temptation to play by ear, which came easily to her. Her childhood music teachers would assign her a new piece and, at her request, play it for her. She would listen and watch intently and then play it the next week with very little practice.

When she arrived at Bob Jones University as a freshman, dreaming of the day she would finally "master the keyboard," Rebecca still did not realize the necessity of detailed practice and classical study. But she soon did. She also came to value form and structure more in composition classes and began to take a "compositional approach" to hymn arranging. She went on to graduate school at BJU, earning a master's degree, and became a member of the music faculty. During her sixteen years in that capacity, she taught, played for chapel, organized the music for Bible Conferences, wrote and arranged music, and played for Vespers choirs and numerous recitals.

Now living in Texas, Rebecca teaches music lessons and serves as music director and pianist for her home church. She also writes and arranges music. Her manuscripts (which currently number over two hundred) include original compositions, vocal art songs, instrumental works, and sacred choral pieces for SATB, SAB, SSA, TTBB, and TTB. Many of these are published by SoundForth.

Her life verse is Psalm 37:23—"The steps of a good man are ordered by the Lord." She says, "I have kept that verse in mind all during college and even today as I think on the importance of staying in the will of God and allowing Him to guide me."

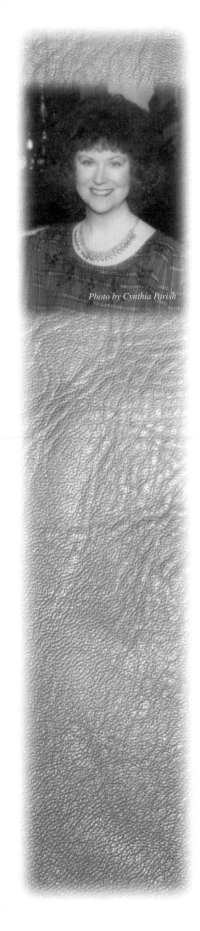

Photo by Cynthia Parish

The Old-Time Religion

Traditional Melody
Arranged by Rebecca Bonam

Whiter Than Snow

William G. Fischer
Arranged by Rebecca Bonam

The Bible Stands

Haldor Lillenas
Arranged by Rebecca Bonam

Dwelling in Beulah Land

C. Austin Miles
Arranged by Rebecca Bonam

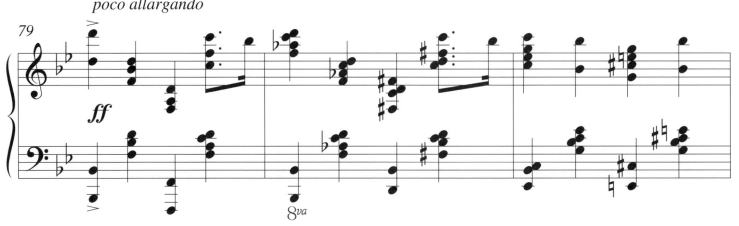

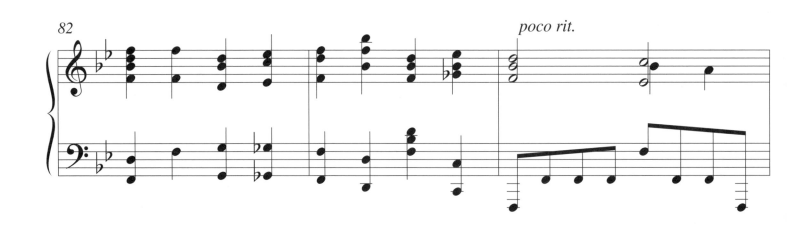

Walking in the King's Highway

Florence Horton
Arranged by Rebecca Bonam

The Great Physician

J. H. Stockton
Arranged by Rebecca Bonam

Come, Thou Fount

Traditional
Arranged by Rebecca Bonam

Precious Lord, Take My Hand

Thomas Dorsey
Arranged by Rebecca Bonam

It Took A Miracle

John W. Peterson
Arranged by Rebecca Bonam

His Eye Is on the Sparrow

Charles H. Gabriel
Arranged by Rebecca Bonam

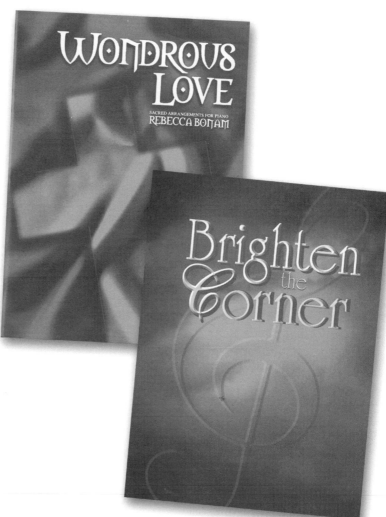

HOW FIRM A FOUNDATION
Sacred Arrangements for Piano
This long-awaited collection brings you seven fresh sacred arrangements
featuring the distinctive style of Rebecca Bonam. *Advanced.*
103184 How Firm a Foundation   Call for price.

HOW FIRM A FOUNDATION
Sacred Arrangements for Piano
This recording by Rebecca Bonam includes all twelve arrangements featured in
the "How Firm a Foundation" and "Wondrous Love" collections. A great recording
for inspiration and listening enjoyment.
112607 CD   Call for price.
112615 Cassette   Call for price.

WONDROUS LOVE
Sacred Arrangements for Piano
Five beautiful, advanced-level piano solos arranged by Rebecca Bonam. Included
on the *How Firm a Foundation* CD.
113555 Book   Call for price.

BRIGHTEN THE CORNER
Sacred Arrangements for Piano
Third in a series of outstanding piano collections from Rebecca Bonam, "Brighten
the Corner" is designed to be accessible to the intermediate player.
116624 Book   Call for price.

SOUNDFORTH 1-800-258-7288

Index